The Joseph Code

A Success Formula for Men

Reclaim Masculinity Mission and
the Strength to Lead with God

Written by David Pixley Traino

Published by Alessia Books

The Joseph Code: A Success Formula for Men

Published by Alessia Books
© 2025 by David Pixley Traino
Printed in the United States of America
All rights reserved.

ISBN: 978-1-967704-04-0

Cover design, editing, and illustrations by
Alexis Traino and David Traino

www.saintly-inspirations.com

THE JOSEPH CODE

TABLE OF CONTENTS

www.saintly-inspirations.com

Introduction

The Joseph Code was created as a companion to the book *Saintly Inspirations: St. Joseph A Bold Model of Manhood for a World in Crisis*. That book explores the life of St. Joseph as a true model of what it means to be a man—faithful, strong, silent in pride but bold in purpose.

After finishing the book, I realized something essential: the message had to be taken further. It had to be made personal.

The truth is that many men today feel adrift.

The world has turned manhood into a moving target— either toxic, disposable, or irrelevant.

Young men are growing up without a clear idea of who they are supposed to become, what role they are meant to fill, or how to build a life that truly matters.

Some are stuck. Some are angry. Some are just numb.

I am writing this guide for you.

This isn't a lecture or a motivational gimmick. It's a short, direct, and powerful tool designed to help you reflect on the kind of man you want to become —and how to get there.

Through the example of St. Joseph, we examine what it means to be a true provider, protector, and spiritual leader, not in some outdated sense, but in a way that restores meaning, direction, and strength to your life.

You've probably heard it a thousand times: "You can be anything you want to be." It's a nice idea, and there's truth to it—your future is wide open.

But if we're being real, not everyone gets to be an NBA star, a tech billionaire, or the next internet sensation. Every one of us has unique strengths and real limitations. That's just life.

But here's the good news—there's one thing every man can work toward, regardless of background or starting point: a life that is genuinely meaningful, productive, and at peace with who you are.

That's not about a job title, a bank account, or likes on a post. It's about the quality of your days and the purpose you carry, whatever your path looks like.

That's the one kind of greatness that's actually within everyone's reach—if you're willing to take it seriously.

You don't need to be perfect.

You just need to be willing to start. St. Joseph shows us that real greatness comes not from applause or power, but from faithfulness, sacrifice, and a purpose-driven life.

God gave you free will.

The next move is yours.

My challenge to you is simple:
Take this guide and test it.

Measure it against the noise you hear every day.

Compare it to what the world is offering you right now—hookup culture, self-glorification, directionless pleasure, endless scrolling.

Ask yourself: Is any of that building me into the man I was meant to be?

You have the power to choose the kind of man you'll become.

No one—least of all me—can do that for you.

But if you give this a real shot, if you lean in with an open heart, you might discover something different.

Something deeper.

You might just uncover a forgotten blueprint for manhood that still holds the power to change everything.

It's called *The Joseph Code*.

A code of masculinity rooted in faith.
Formed in silence. Fueled by sacrifice.

A code of mission, clarity, and strength—with God at the center.

So try it.

Not just as a book—but as a test. As a challenge. As a code to live by. Because if it's real—*really real*—it will stand up to anything this world throws at you.

This isn't just a guide.

It's a spark.
A mirror.
And maybe… your map.

Read it slowly.
Reflect deeply.

And decide for yourself:

Is this the code you've been searching for?

OPENING PRAYER

Lord God,

In a world that often mocks manhood or tries to erase it, I come to You seeking truth. I am tired of confusion, of pressure to perform without purpose, of living without clear direction. I want more. I want to become the man You created me to be—not perfect, but faithful. Not loud, but strong. Not self-centered, but self-giving.

Teach me through the life of St. Joseph—his quiet courage, his steady hand, his trust in You, even when nothing made sense. Give me the strength to lead with love, to protect without pride, and to provide with integrity.

Help me reject what is shallow and chase what is eternal. I know that becoming a man of God is not easy, but it is worth everything. Form me. Guide me. Lord, take my hand and walk with me. I cannot do this alone.

Amen.

THE CRISIS OF
MANHOOD

This isn't just a problem. It's a silent collapse—and it's happening all around us. You may not see it on the surface. No one is holding signs.

There's no emergency alert. But look deeper—and you'll feel it: A generation of young men quietly drowning in confusion, anger, and isolation. And the culture? It just shrugs.

It either mocks masculinity or ignores it altogether.
It offers no answers. No direction.
Just noise.

THE FALLOUT: DISCONNECTED. DISCOURAGED. DIRECTIONLESS.

Young men today are facing a storm unlike anything in recent history.

-Record levels of anxiety, depression, and addiction.
-Plummeting school achievement and work participation.
-Fewer marriages. Fewer fathers. Fewer men leading well.
-More isolation. More screens. More apathy.
-Less purpose. Less strength. Less clarity.

You've been told to be strong—but not too strong.

To speak up—but not offend.
To lead—but not lead too boldly.
To be sensitive—but never struggle.
To be a man—but... not that kind of man.

So what happens?
Men check out. Or they blow up.
They become passive shadows—or angry shells.
Neither one becomes who he's meant to be.

THE CONFUSION:
TODAY'S CULTURE IS LYING TO YOU

The world has fed you a broken blueprint:

"You don't need responsibility. Just experience."
"You don't need a purpose. Just pleasure."
"You don't need a woman. Just options."
"You don't need faith. Just confidence."
"You don't need discipline. Just vibes."

But here's the cold reality:

This model of manhood isn't just failing—it's destroying lives.

It's why so many men are emotionally numb, spiritually empty, and relationally lost.

Why we see broken homes, abandoned children, and wasted potential.

Why a generation is sleepwalking into manhood without a map—and crashing hard.

And behind it all, one aching, unspoken question beats in the soul of so many:

"Am I enough?"

THE MISSION: MANHOOD MUST BE RECOVERED

Manhood doesn't just happen. It's not automatic.

You don't wake up one day and suddenly know who you are.

It must be taught. Modeled. Transmitted.

And most of all, it must be chosen.

It's time to stop absorbing culture's confusion and start building something different.

Something older than social media. Stronger than broken systems.

Deeper than a podcast clip or a trending post.

We need examples of greatness. Not rooted in arrogance or dominance—but in sacrifice, strength, clarity, and self-control.

And there's no better place to start than with the man God handpicked to raise His Son.

That's why St. Joseph matters.

He was a man of silence and power.

Of humility and resolve.

Of courage, protection, purity, and obedience.

He was what modern manhood has forgotten. And what this generation desperately needs to recover.

This guide is about reclaiming that blueprint.

Not with guilt trips or lectures—but with clarity, truth, and a real path forward.

You don't have to wander anymore.

You don't have to guess at who to be.

You can choose a formula for success.

Be the man God created you to become.

Start now.

Before the world finishes the job of unmaking you.

A WARNING
TO MEN

Let's not sugarcoat it. There is a war being waged for your soul, and most young men have no idea they're in the middle of it.

This war isn't fought with guns or soldiers. It's fought in silence, on screens, in bedrooms, and hearts.

It's a war of distraction, disorientation, and despair. And it is destroying a generation of men before they've even had the chance to become one.

The world doesn't care if you fail. In fact, culture and even governments benefit when you stay weak, passive, addicted, and confused.

Why?

Because a man who doesn't know who he is—who doesn't know his mission, his purpose, or his God—is easy to control.

Easy to sell to. Easy to silence. Easy to waste.

Here is the truth no one may have told you:

The biggest threat to your future is not other people. It's the slow erosion of your soul through comfort, compromise, and confusion.

Let's name the traps:

- **Passivity**: You stop showing up. You let life happen to you. You avoid the hard questions. You drift. You scroll. You waste time. And you call it "freedom."

- **Pride**: You build an image but have no foundation. You pretend to have answers but never seek the truth. You make everything about yourself and end up empty.

- **Pornography and Lust**: You train your heart to consume, not to love. You numb your spirit to real intimacy and sabotage your future relationships before they begin.

- **Isolation**: You cut yourself off from mentors, community, and God. You say "I'm fine" when you're drowning. You laugh while your spirit is bleeding out.

These are not just bad habits. These are spiritual weapons.

They kill purpose.
They kill discipline.
They kill marriages before they start.

They turn potential husbands and fathers into wandering boys with no compass.

But here's the good news: you can wake up. You can fight back. It's your choice to become something different.

You don't have to have it all figured out. You don't have to be perfect. But you do have to take ownership. You do have to choose a side.

You were made to lead, to protect, to build, to love, and to worship. If you don't fight for that future, someone or something will take it from you.

Your decisions right now—yes, right now—are forming the kind of man you are becoming.

That's not fear. That's reality.

Ask yourself honestly:

- **Am I preparing to be a husband or avoiding real commitment?**

- **Am I pursuing purity or settling for fake love behind a screen?**

- **Am I building a life or just reacting to it?**

- **Am I walking with God or pretending He'll still be there when I'm finally ready?**

Yes, it's hard to face this. But so is regret. So is watching your future collapse because you refused to confront your present.

This isn't about shame. This is about clarity.

It's your life. It's your future.

If you're ready to fight back, start by naming the lies.

Because before you can become the man God created you to be...

You
need to
see
clearly
what's
been
holding
you back.

WHAT THEY TOLD YOU ABOUT MANHOOD IS A LIE

7 CULTURAL TRAPS TO REJECT

In a culture that claims to celebrate authenticity, young men are constantly being fed a false, distorted image of what manhood is supposed to look like. It's no wonder so many feel lost. The confusion isn't your fault, but staying in it is your choice.

Below are seven central lies promoted by our modern secular culture shaping modern manhood—**and the truth that will set you free.**

LIE #1: "MASCULINITY IS TOXIC"

The attack on manhood is not subtle anymore. It's full-blown, relentless, and devastating.

In today's culture, you'll hear it everywhere: masculinity is the problem. If men would stop being men, the world would be better off. Turn on a sitcom, scroll through social media, or sit in a college lecture hall, and you'll hear it in a thousand ways— some loud, some disguised in humor or politics.

The message is clear: manhood is dangerous. Manhood is oppressive. Manhood is optional.

And sadly, a generation of young men is absorbing that message. Silently. Shamefully.

Let's be honest: some men have done real damage through abuse, aggression, and abandonment.

THE ANSWER TO BROKEN MASCULINITY ISN'T TO ERASE IT.
IT'S TO REDEEM IT.
THE PROBLEM ISN'T MASCULINITY.
THE PROBLEM IS MASCULINITY WITHOUT VIRTUE.

THE TRUTH: MASCULINITY IS NOT TOXIC—IT'S SACRED

God designed men with strength, not to dominate, but to serve.

He designed men to lead, not for control, but for courageous responsibility.

He wired men to protect, build, sacrifice, and bring life to others.

This isn't theory. It's built into your DNA. You were made to be a provider, protector, and spiritual leader. You were never meant to be passive, isolated, or ashamed of your design.

Real masculinity—like we see in St. Joseph—is humble, faithful, and unshakably strong.

He never spoke a word in Scripture, yet his actions protected the Holy Family, provided for them in exile, and led them through uncertainty. Joseph was not weak. He was a giant in silence.

You don't need to apologize for being a man. You need to step into what that truly means.

THE CULTURAL CONFUSION: LIES THAT ARE LEAVING YOUNG MEN HOLLOW

Culture tells you to blend in. Suppress your instinct to lead. Mute your drive to provide. Numb out your emotions. Unplug your sense of mission.

You're told that:
- **Strong women are empowering, but strong men are threatening.**
- **Girls should be fierce, but boys should sit down and behave.**
- **Gender is fluid, roles are outdated, and tradition is dangerous.**

The result? A generation of men with no identity, no direction, and no idea how to form meaningful relationships.

As a recent Wall Street Journal article described: "Many young men are simply failing to launch." They're falling behind in school, avoiding marriage, addicted to screens and escapism, disconnected from faith, and quietly desperate for meaning.

At Life Tabernacle Church in Baton Rouge, they saw it firsthand: boys growing up without fathers, men growing up without a mission. What turned it around? Clear spiritual structure. Masculine mentorship. A community that didn't shame manhood—it called it forth.

And it worked. Because young men don't want to be erased, they want to be needed.

THE BIBLICAL MODEL: PARTNERSHIP, NOT COMPETITION

You were not made to compete with women. You were made to complement them.

From the very beginning, God designed a man and a woman, not as rivals, but as a pair. Each was made in His image. Each with distinct gifts. Each is incomplete without the other.

You were wired for a relationship. For the covenant. For communion.

Our culture has tried to erase this reality—to flatten all differences, remove all roles, and deny the very structure of creation. But that denial hasn't brought freedom; it's brought confusion, anxiety, bitterness, and deep loneliness.

Why? Because freedom without structure is not empowerment, it's disorientation.

It often brings disorder and chaos. We aren't meant to have unbridled freedom. Our brains and our DNA have evolved over thousands of years within inherent structures that have guided our daily lives.

Yes, you can try to engineer our lives socially, but the truth is that there are strong biological factors that often come into conflict with these otherwise well-meaning attempts.

Modern culture and society offer a glimpse into the unintended consequences of denying this reality.

When men stop being men and women stop being women, the beauty of life falls apart.

We need each other. We were made for each other.

YOUR MOVE: REDEEM MANHOOD. DON'T APOLOGIZE—LIVE IT BOLDLY

You were not made to be ashamed of your strength. You were made to use it.

To build. To bless. To rise.

If you've ever felt like something was off in what you're being told, trust that instinct.

It's not just you. It's the truth rising up inside of you.

- **Embrace the quiet strength of Joseph.**
- **Respect women by earning their trust and demonstrating leadership.**
- **Lead with conviction, not control.**
- **Love with purpose, not performance.**
- **Be bold. Be clean. Be unapologetically male—and radically holy.**

You were made for this. The world may reject it. But heaven is cheering you on and you will be better for it.

REFLECTION QUESTIONS:

- When have I felt unsure or even ashamed of my masculinity? Where did that message come from?
- What role models of manhood have shaped me, for better or worse?
- How can I begin to reclaim the confidence and clarity of being a man formed by God?

LIE #2: "EMOTIONS MAKE YOU WEAK"

Real men don't cry. Real men don't talk. Real men bury it and move on... right? That's the message you've been sold.

Boys are told from a young age:
- **"Suck it up."**
- **"Don't be soft."**
- **"Get over it."**

So you learned early: pain gets stuffed. Fear gets silenced. Tears get swallowed. You didn't stop feeling. You just stopped sharing. And that silence became your prison. The world told you to be "stoic"—but what it really meant was numb. And numbness, over time, doesn't make you stronger. It makes you colder, harder, and lonelier.

THE TRUTH: EMOTION IS NOT THE OPPOSITE OF STRENGTH-IT'S PART OF IT

You were created in God's image. And the very author of masculinity is not emotionally repressed. **Jesus wept.**

He got angry.
He rejoiced.
He agonized.
He sweat blood.
He shouted in victory.
He grieved over friends and mourned over cities.

So what kind of lie tells you that feeling deeply makes you less of a man? True manhood isn't found in emotional suppression.
It's found in emotional mastery. That means you don't let your feelings control you, but you also don't pretend they don't exist.
You bring them to God. You process them with maturity. You act, not react.

That's not weakness. That's power under control.

THE CULTURAL LIE: SHUT UP AND STAY ANGRY

Today's culture is a mess of emotional contradictions.

On one hand, it glorifies unhinged emotion, rage videos, Twitter rants, and emotional outbursts.

On the other hand, it mocks men who express their vulnerability with dignity.

So most men live in quiet confusion:

- **If you share too much, you're weak.**
- **If you share nothing, you're toxic.**
- **If you're angry, you're dangerous.**
- **If you're sad, you're unstable.**

No wonder you feel trapped.

But here's the truth: silence doesn't heal anything. It only hardens the wound.

And wounded men wound others.

Do you want to be a better man? Stop hiding. Start healing.
Do you want to love a woman someday? Learn how to express yourself now.

Do you want to lead a family? Start by leading your own heart to wholeness.

THE ANGER TRAP—WHY SUPPRESSING FEELINGS TURNS TO RAGE

Here's a hard truth: most men aren't taught to deal with the full range of emotions—fear, shame, sadness, disappointment. Instead, we're trained from boyhood to bottle them up until only one emotion remains: *anger*. Anger becomes the one feeling society "permits" men to show. It's the steam valve, the default setting. It is sometimes glorified in movies.

But here's what rarely gets said: anger is often just the mask that covers up everything else you aren't allowed to express.

- **Sad? That turns to anger.**
- **Hurt? Anger.**
- **Ashamed or afraid? More anger.**

And here's the twist: the very emotion you're "allowed" to show as a man is the one most demonized by the world.

So you're left with two options: anger and rage, or numbness. Both are prisons. Both leave you isolated.

Suppressing your emotions doesn't protect you; it disconnects you from your own heart. Over time, that chronic anger isn't just about the world outside you; it's about everything you never gave yourself permission to feel or say. And unaddressed, it will leak out as frustration, bitterness, or even violence, hurting those you care about most.

Authentic manhood isn't about bottling up or blowing up. It's about facing what you feel and learning to lead through it. Anger is just one emotion; it isn't the only one, and it was never meant to be your whole story.

THE MODEL: JOSEPH AND THE STRENGTH OF STEADINESS

Joseph doesn't say a word in Scripture, but that doesn't mean he was emotionally dead.

Imagine his life:
- The scandal of Mary's pregnancy.
- The fear of fleeing to Egypt.
- The burden of protecting the Messiah from a king who wanted Him dead.

Do you think Joseph never trembled? Never questioned? Never feared?

Of course he did. But instead of shutting down, he stayed steady.

His emotions didn't paralyze him; they propelled him to obedience.

He didn't act out of panic. He acted from prayer.

That's manhood.

YOUR MOVE: FACE WHAT YOU FEEL. THEN LEAD THROUGH IT.

You want to grow up? Stop pretending you're fine.

Talk to someone. Write it down. Pray it out.

Bring the emotions into the light—before they explode in the dark.

Here's the challenge:

- **Start journaling once a week.**

- **Confess one hidden pain to your priest, mentor, or close friend.**

- **Name your emotions to God—say them out loud in prayer.**

- **Don't get stuck between rage and numbness.**

There is another way: the path of quiet strength, clear vision, and healed manhood.

REFLECTION QUESTIONS:

- What emotion do I hide the most—and why?
- When was the last time I felt something deeply and didn't bury it?
- Who do I trust enough to be real with?

"The Lord is near to the brokenhearted and saves those who are crushed in spirit." — Psalm 34:18

LIE #3: "YOUR VALUE IS BASED ON SUCCESS AS OTHERS DEFINE IT"

What is your worth? The world has an answer: Only as much as you can prove to others.

From your earliest years, the scoreboard is set:
How much money do you make?
How impressive is your title?

How many people follow you, like your post, or admire your brand?

The message? Your value is transactional. Perform well— you're worthy. Fall behind—you're invisible.

This is the gospel of hustle culture. And it's making men miserable.

We live in an era where the grind never seems to end. You're told: "Work harder. Be more. Own more. Post more. Win more."

And the moment you stop—even to breathe—you feel like you're falling behind.

But here's the truth:

You were not made to be a machine. You were made to be a man.

THE TRUTH: YOUR VALUE COMES FROM GOD, NOT FROM METRICS

Before you ever made a dollar, won a game, earned a title, or attracted an audience, God loved you.

Before you even had the chance to perform or impress anyone, He saw your soul and called it good.

You were created in the image of God. Not the algorithm. Not the marketplace. Not the comments section.

A man of integrity, shaped by quiet discipline and strong faith, is worth more than a thousand hollow influencers.

St. Joseph never went viral. He was never rich. He left no writings. He held no title beyond "carpenter."

But he was entrusted with the Son of God and the Mother of the Church. That's who God trusts—not the self-promoter, but the selfless.

Joseph built in silence. He served without applause. He showed us the dignity of quiet work, steady character, and purpose lived daily, without a crowd.

That is real success.

THE CULTURAL LIE: HUSTLE OVER HOLINESS

Culture wants you to chase the image, not the soul.

It tells you to build a platform, not a life.

To grind until you burn out—and then shame you for needing rest.

Social media has convinced millions of young men that value is tied to:

- Owning luxury you can't afford

- Flexing achievements you haven't earned

- Pretending to have a life you can't sustain

You end up comparing your real life to everyone else's highlight reel, and it leaves you exhausted, anxious, and ashamed.

But here's the reality no one posts about:

Half of the "success" you admire online is empty, performative, and built on debt or dysfunction.

THE SUCCESS TRAP—HOW EXTERNAL VALIDATION AND ATTENTION HIJACK YOUR LIFE

Here's the trap:

When your attention is always pointed outward—checking likes, chasing applause, scrolling for someone else's approval, you become blind to your real worth.

You start to believe the only things that matter are what others see, rate, and applaud. **This is called *attention externalization:* you lose the habit of checking in with your own heart and start living for the next notification.**

The mind's natural state is to seek meaning and direction from within, but technology, hustle culture, and social comparison constantly pull your focus outside yourself.

This relentless search for validation leaves you restless, insecure, and always chasing the next hit of approval. It is a treadmill you can never get off.

External validation is a moving target.

- **The moment you reach one goal, the goalpost moves.**
- **There is always someone with more followers, a better job, or a bigger trophy.**
- **You are trained to measure yourself against what you see, not who you really are.**

The problem?
When you build your life on other people's applause, you lose the ability to know what actually makes you come alive.

You become a product, not a person.

Men who live for external validation become exhausted and empty inside.

True fulfillment never comes from performing for the crowd. It comes from living out of your God-given identity and mission, regardless of who's watching.

Freedom begins when you reclaim your attention and worth from the world—and hand them back to God.

The Biblical Model: Success = Faithfulness

God never asked Joseph to be famous. He asked him to be faithful.

God never demanded perfection—just obedience. God never required credentials—just courage.

God didn't choose His only son's earthly father based on resume or social standing.

He chose a man whose heart was aligned with heaven. That's what God wants from you—not flash, but faithfulness.

Your income does not define you.
Your GPA does not define you.

You are not defined by the girl who rejected you, the boss who overlooked you, or the post that didn't get liked.

You are defined by who you belong to, and the man you are becoming on the inside.

YOUR MOVE: BUILD FROM THE INSIDE OUT

We need to be clear about one thing. You still need to work hard. Excellence matters. Responsibility matters. Working hard and making sacrifices are part of reality for most people. That will never change.

But it's not the world's applause you're chasing. It's God's well done.

And here's the truth: real manhood demands everything from you.

Not everything the world demands, but everything God placed inside you.

Your drive, your energy, your creativity, your focus—these are gifts. They're not meant to lie dormant.

You were made to build, to stretch, to struggle, and to strive.

But not to be someone else.

You were made to become the best version of the man God created you to be.

You don't need to be taller, richer, faster, or louder.

You don't need a bigger platform or more likes.

What you need is to wake up every day with a commitment to honor the unique set of talents, strengths, and challenges that God has given you, no one else.

This means:

- **Don't settle. If you're coasting, you're wasting.**
- **Push yourself—not to impress others—but to unleash what God wired into your soul.**
- **Be relentless—not in comparison, but in personal obedience and purpose.**
- **Work hard because your life matters, not because you need to beat anyone else.**

Your success will look different from someone else's—and that's not just okay, that's divine design.

Culture misses an important truth.

Chasing the "find your passion myth" is a distraction. Don't buy it. You were meant to do something, maybe only one thing, really, really well.

Find that and make that your passion. Because chasing feelings won't get you anywhere, but building something real will.

What matters is that you use what you've been given, wholeheartedly, faithfully, and with joy.

Whether you're shaping wood like Joseph, fixing diesel engines, starting a business, coaching kids, or leading prayer, do it like a man who knows it matters.

REFLECTION QUESTIONS:

- Do I tie my self-worth to what I achieve? Where did that belief come from?
- How do I act when I'm not achieving anything? Who am I when I'm not performing?
- Am I building a soul... or just a résumé?

God will never ask you why you weren't someone else.

He will ask why you weren't fully you.

The world says, "Be impressive."

God says, "Be whole."

Only one of those voices leads to peace.

LIE #4: "SEX IS JUST A GAME"

You were made to love. But the world taught you to consume.

Look around. Sex is everywhere. It's marketed, streamed, joked about, and expected. The message couldn't be clearer: Sex is casual. Sex is currency. Sex is entertainment.

And if you're not having it or at least fantasizing about it constantly, you're missing out.

That's what they tell you.

But behind the laughter and the marketing, here's what they don't show you:

- **The dead eyes of addiction.**
- **The shame of secrecy.**
- **The hollow feeling after casual hookups.**
- **The brokenness left in a heart trained to take, not give.**

This isn't about being prudish or afraid of sexuality. This is about truth.

Sex isn't just a physical act—it's a spiritual one. A soul-deep bond.

And when you treat something sacred like it's disposable, you get hurt—and you hurt others.

THE TRUTH: SEX IS HOLY—NOT RECREATIONAL

God created sex, not Hollywood. Not porn. Not hookup culture. And He designed it to be wildly powerful, within a lifelong covenant of love and for the purpose of procreation.

Sex is meant to seal a promise. To express something permanent.
It's a physical echo of a spiritual reality: I belong to you, and only you, forever.

The Bible is clear: sex is a gift reserved for marriage between a man and a woman.

That's not just an old rule—it's God's blueprint for love that lasts.

Culture might say it doesn't matter, but ignoring this leads to brokenness, regret, and wounds we never meant to carry.

When we honor God's design, we open the door to the kind of love, trust, and joy that was meant to last a lifetime.

That's why it's so devastating when misused.

Every image you consume, every casual experience you pursue outside of that context, isn't just a "mistake."

It's a misformation of your soul. You're teaching your heart that people are objects. You're training your body for disconnection instead of communion.

And worst of all? You're weakening your ability to give and receive love the way God designed it.

THE CULTURAL LIE: "IT'S JUST PHYSICAL"

No, it's not. And you know it.

If sex were just physical, pornography wouldn't destroy relationships. If it were just physical, hookups wouldn't leave people emptier than before.

If it were just physical, people wouldn't carry sexual wounds for a lifetime. The truth is: what you do with your body affects who you are becoming.

But everyone does it. It's the culture. So why can't I? Because:

- **Porn rewires your brain.**
- **Hookup culture numbs your heart.**
- **Lust turns love into a lie.**

And men today are drowning in it. Good men.

Young men. Church-going men. Because no one told them that fighting for purity isn't weakness—it's warfare for your future.

THE MODEL: JOSEPH AND MARY

St. Joseph was engaged to the most beautiful and holy woman in history.
And yet he chose restraint, reverence, and righteousness.

He didn't push boundaries—he protected them.
He didn't use Mary. He covered her in honor.
What would your relationships look like if you treated every woman like that?

What would your future marriage look like if you started preparing now, not by taking, but by cherishing?

YOUR MOVE: LIVE PURE. LOVE STRONG.

Purity isn't repression. It's power under control.
It's saying

- **"I'm not going to let lust rule me."**

- **"I'm not going to use women, even in my thoughts."**

- **"I'm not going to bond with a screen—I'm preparing my soul for a real woman."**

This is hard. You will struggle.

But every fight for purity is a fight for your future wife, your future kids, and your future peace.

The world will laugh. But they're not the ones who will live with your consequences.

You are.

So fight like a man.

REFLECTION QUESTIONS:

- Have I allowed lust or porn to steal my ability to love?
- Do I treat women as souls to be protected, or as objects to be used?
- What's one habit I need to end, and one boundary I need to build today?

"Your body isn't your own. It was bought at a price. So honor God with it." (1 Corinthians 6:19-20)

BATTLE PLAN FOR PURITY

Fight for your soul, your future marriage, and your peace of mind.

If you're going to win the war for purity, you need more than a good intention.

You need a strategy. A structure. A plan of action.

This isn't about being perfect. It's about training like a man who takes his soul seriously.

Step 1: Name the Real Enemy

Lust isn't just a feeling. It's a spiritual enemy—and it plays dirty.
Lust promises pleasure but leaves you emptier every time.

Porn trains you to be a consumer, not a protector. Compromise starts small but rots everything from the inside out.

You don't defeat the enemy by pretending it's not that bad.
Call it what it is. Then choose to fight.

Step 2: Know Your Triggers

Every temptation has a pattern. Get to know yours.

Ask yourself:

- **When am I most tempted? (late at night, when I'm tired, alone, etc.)**
- **What situations weaken my resolve?**
- **What thoughts start the spiral?**

Awareness is power. When you see it coming, you can choose a different response.

Step 3: Set Unbreakable Boundaries

You can't outpray what you won't outsmart.

Set non-negotiable limits in your daily life:

- **No phone in bed at night.**
- **No browsing without a purpose.**
- **Use filtering software like Covenant Eyes or Ever Accountable.**
- **Get rid of private access to temptation—yes, even if it's inconvenient.**

Freedom requires fences. Don't wait to fall before you build them.

Step 4: Bring it Into the Light

Lust grows in silence.

Purity grows in brotherhood.

You cannot win this battle alone.

Talk to someone you trust, such as a mentor, pastor, friend, or accountability partner.

Say the words. Confess the struggle.

Let someone walk with you—and remind you you're not the only one in the fight.

Shame dies when stories are shared.

Step 5: Replace, Don't Just Resist

You can't just say "no" to lust—you have to say "yes" to something better.

Fill your time and heart with things that feed your soul:

- **Work out. With weights. Get strong.**
- **Serve others.**
- **Pursue a creative project.**
- **Spend time with real people.**
- **Read, pray, build.**

Lust will knock louder when your life feels empty.
Fill it with purpose, and the noise fades.

Step 6: Fight Spiritually, Not Just Mentally

This isn't just about discipline—it's about dependence on God.

Ask Him daily:

"Lord, cleanse my eyes. Guard my heart. Let me see women as You see them—and prepare me to love as You love."

Ideas for the spiritual fight:
- **Fast once a week.**
- **Pray before bed.**
- **Use Scripture as a sword— "Blessed are the pure in heart, for they shall see God." (Matthew 5:8)**

Step 7: Start a Streak Today

Lay out a spiritual plan for yourself and then commit to it.

One day.
Then two.
Then a week.
Then a month.

If you fall? Don't quit. Get back up. That's how men grow.

You are not fighting against pleasure.

You are fighting for purity, for joy, and for the kind of love that's worth everything.

LIE #5: "WOMEN ARE A DISTRACTION OR A COMMODITY"

They're either in the way of your dreams or here to serve your desires. Either way, they're not your equal; they're your problem.

That's the lie whispered in everything from locker rooms to music videos.

It says:

- Women are emotional, needy, and dramatic.
- They're either too much or not enough.
- They're obstacles to your mission or prizes to be won.
- They're tools for your pleasure or voices to be ignored.

And if you believe that, even a little, you're not only dishonoring them—you're destroying yourself.

Because how you view women shapes your soul.
And your future.

THE CULTURAL TRUTH: YOU'RE BEING TRAINED TO USE WOMEN

Every ad, movie, show, and scroll trains your brain: women are images, not persons.

- You swipe through faces like apps.
- You click on bodies like products.
- You laugh at "jokes" that dehumanize them.
- You scroll through influencers pretending it's entertainment.

And over time, something inside you changes:

You stop seeing women as sacred.

You stop believing in love.

You start believing the lie that intimacy is a game, not a gift.

You become numb.

You want more, but feel less.

You crave connection, but lose the ability to offer it.

And then one day, you try to love a real woman, and you realize you have no idea how.

THE REAL TRUTH: WOMEN ARE NOT THE PROBLEM—THEY'RE PART OF THE MISSION

God didn't create women to be your toy, your opponent, or your inconvenience.

He created her as a partner, a gift, and a reflection of His own heart.

"Then the Lord God said, 'It is not good for the man to be alone.'" (Genesis 2:18)

Manhood wasn't complete without womanhood.

God's plan for your strength is tied directly to how you honor, protect, and cherish women.

You were not made to conquer women.
You were made to lift them.

That means:
- **Speak with honor.**
- **Think with reverence.**
- **Love with purity.**
- **Lead with humility.**

THE MODEL: JOSEPH'S RADICAL HONOR

Joseph had every legal right to abandon Mary when he discovered she was pregnant.

He could have saved his reputation and walked away. Let her face public shame.

But he didn't.

YOUR MOVE: SEE HER AS HEAVEN SEES HER

Every woman you see is someone's daughter.

Every woman is made in the image of God.

Every woman has a soul, a story, and a calling.

So stop scrolling past their dignity.

Stop speaking about them like objects.

You want to be different? Then act differently.

- **Speak truth, not trash.**
- **Confess when your thoughts drift into objectification.**
- **Stop watching anything that teaches you to see women as less.**
- **Start praying for the women around you—not just the one you hope to marry someday.**

This world needs men who don't use women, mock women, or fear women. It needs men who will protect, bless, listen, and love.

REFLECTION QUESTIONS:

- How has culture trained me to see women? Consider several ways in which modern culture and media distort your view of women.
- Do I honor women with my thoughts, my eyes, my words?
- What's one way I can show more respect and care for the women in my life, starting today?

The bible tells us to treat "older women as mothers, younger women as sisters, with all purity." — 1 Timothy 5:2

LIE #6: "FAITH IS FOR THE WEAK"

Belief is for soft men. Strong men don't need God—they build their own destiny.

That's the cultural mantra.

It tells you real men are "self-made." That faith is a crutch. That prayer is wishful thinking. That obedience is cowardice. That church is for women, kids, and weaklings.

So you keep your faith hidden. Or distant.

You may show up at Mass. You may even say you believe.
But the fire? The conviction? The boldness?

Somewhere along the way, it got buried under the pressure to be "normal."

But listen carefully: that pressure is killing your soul.
The world says men should be fearless—but then ridicules the very faith that builds unshakable courage.

THE TRUTH: FAITH IS THE FIERCEST STRENGTH A MAN CAN HAVE

Jesus didn't die to make you passive.

He died to wake you up, to set you free, to give you purpose, and to make you dangerous to the darkness.

Faith isn't a backup plan. It's the battle plan.

The saints weren't mild.

They were warriors of the spirit. Builders of nations. Slayers of sin. They faced death, rejection, persecution, and ridicule—and they stood firm because their strength didn't come from the world. It came from above.

Faith is not fragile. It's ferocious.
It means you no longer live for the crowd.

You live for the King.

THE CULTURAL LIE: RELIGION IS CONTROL, NOT FREEDOM

Today's voices love to mock religion.

They say it's outdated. Oppressive. Superstitious. Narrow. But ask yourself:

Is the world you see full of joy?

Are the influencers and celebrities you follow truly fulfilled? Are the men you know who mock faith living lives of peace, purpose, and courage?

Or are they lost, anxious, addicted, aimless?
The truth is this: without God, men break.

Without something greater than themselves to live for, they drift—or implode.

You weren't made to be your own god.

You were made to bow before the real one—and become unstoppable in His hands.

THE MODEL: JOSEPH'S FAITH MOVED MOUNTAINS

Joseph never gave a public sermon.

He didn't perform miracles.
He didn't write letters to churches or lead great armies.

But when God spoke, he obeyed without hesitation.
He took Mary as his wife.

He fled to Egypt to save Jesus.
He provided, protected, and persevered—because he trusted God with everything.

No fanfare. No platform. Just bold, masculine faith in action.
Joseph believed even in the darkest of nights. He followed without proof.

And that obedience changed the course of history.

YOUR MOVE: DON'T BE ASHAMED OF THE FIRE

It's time to stop whispering your faith.

Stop acting like it's a footnote in your life.

Stop living as if God is an accessory instead of your Commander.

You want to change your life? Then make your faith your foundation.

Pray like a warrior. Read Scripture like it's your sword.

Show up at church like you're reporting for battle.

Live in a way that makes demons nervous.

Start by:

- **Committing to daily time with God—even 10 minutes.**
- **Finding a spiritual brotherhood to strengthen you. Strength in numbers.**
- **Standing up when others sit back.**
- **Choosing purity, truth, and courage—every time it costs you something.**

Real faith costs. But fake manhood costs more.

REFLECTION QUESTIONS:

- Where have I made my faith small or hidden?
- Do I believe God actually wants to lead, strengthen, and use me?
- What's one step I can take this week to become bold in faith?

"Keep alert, stand firm in your faith, be courageous, be strong."

1 Corinthians 16:13

LIE #7: "YOU HAVE TIME TO FIGURE IT OUT LATER"

You're young. Chill out. Party now. Hustle later. Get serious when it actually matters.

This lie is everywhere.

It wraps itself in freedom.

It sounds like liberty, but it's a slow death in disguise.

- **"You're only 18. Live a little."**
- **"You're only 22. You don't need a plan."**
- **"You're only 27. Everyone's lost at this age."**

And then one day... you're 33, 40, and more.
Still uncommitted. Still unformed. Still unready.

That voice inside of you that said "later" was never going to let you go.

It just kept moving the finish line. It's a trap!

THE TRUTH: TIME DOESN'T WAIT FOR YOU—IT FORMS YOU

Right now, whether you realize it or not, you're becoming someone.
Every choice is a chisel.
Every habit is a foundation.

Every year, a wall rises around the house of your character.

"Later" is not neutral. It's formation in disguise.

Put it off long enough, and "later" becomes a life.

- **A life of passivity.**
- **A life of delay.**
- **A life of what-ifs and wish-I-hads.**

And the scariest part? The longer you wait to become a man, the harder it gets even to recognize what one looks like.

THE CULTURAL LIE: EXTENDED ADOLESCENCE = FREEDOM

Culture has redefined manhood as something optional—something you try on when you're ready, if ever.

They say:

- **You don't need a real job, just stream.**
- **You don't need a marriage—cohabitate.**
- **You don't need a purpose—just vibes.**
- **You don't need to grow up—just exist.**

And so we have a generation of boys in grown-up bodies, waiting for a thunderclap of maturity that never comes. You have all heard of Peter Pan syndrome.

But manhood doesn't arrive. It's built.

It doesn't strike you one day. You step into it, making one decision at a time each day.

THE MODEL: JOSEPH DIDN'T WAIT TO BE READY

Joseph wasn't "figuring things out." He wasn't on a 10-year journey of self-discovery in the Judean wilderness.

When God called, he moved.

He was ready—not because life was easy, but because his character was forged.

He had habits. He had virtue. He had integrity.

And when the call came—protect Mary, raise Jesus, flee to Egypt—he didn't say,

"Maybe in a few years when I'm more settled."

He obeyed. Immediately. Because he had already become a man.

YOUR MOVE: STEP UP BEFORE YOU THINK YOU'RE READY

You want a different life?

Then stop acting like a child with time to burn and start preparing like a man with a purpose to live.

- **Wake up early.**
- **Take care of your body. Work out. Stay strong.**
- **Make plans.**
- **Set goals.**
- **Learn discipline.**
- **Build your prayer life.**
- **Own your choices.**
- **Think like a husband—even if you're single.**
- **Work like a provider—even if you're still in school.**
- **Act like a leader—even if no one sees it yet**.

You're not waiting for your life to start.

You're in it. Right now.

REFLECTION QUESTIONS:

- What habits am I forming today that are shaping my future?
- Where have I delayed growth, waiting for some magical "later"?
- What's one area of my life I need to take responsibility for starting now?

"Remember your Creator in the days of your youth, before the days of trouble come…" — Ecclesiastes 12:1

PROVIDE.

PROTECT.

LEAD.

The Blueprint of Manhood from the Life of St. Joseph

Let's not overcomplicate it. Three words define what it truly means to be a man. They aren't trendy. They aren't vague. They aren't subject to cultural approval.

They're ancient, tested, and true:

Provide. Protect. Lead.

These three callings are in your DNA as a man—and they're exactly what the world is starving for. You may not be married yet. You may not have children.

But the life you're building today is laying the foundation for who you will become in every role: husband, father, brother, son, leader.

Let's break these down, not as ideas, but as real-life choices you must begin to make now.

PROVIDE: SHOW UP AND BUILD SOMETHING THAT LASTS

Not with wealth, but with showing up consistently.

Not for applause, but for those who depend on you.

Providing isn't about being rich.

It's about being reliable.

It means you show up, especially when it's hard.

You push past the urge to numb out. You stop waiting for someone else to solve things, and you begin building something of your own.

St. Joseph didn't provide riches for his family—he provided his presence, his strength, his sweat. He showed up every single day with a tool in his hand and a purpose in his soul. That's masculinity in action.

Ask Yourself:

- **Do I take ownership of the things I say I care about?**
- **Am I reliable with small things, or do I only show up when it's easy?**
- **What am I doing today that is preparing me to provide for a future family?**

Try This:

- **Set a consistent wake-up time. Discipline begins in the morning. Make your bed every day.**
- **Commit to one hard thing this week you've been avoiding—then do it.**
- **Start tracking your time: Are you building something, or escaping?**

To earn respect, you must shoulder responsibility.

It's not a burden. It's your mission.

PROTECT: STAND IN THE GAP —EVEN WHEN IT COSTS YOU

Not by force, but by protective courage.

Not by dominance, but by faithful strength and calm conviction.

Protection isn't just physical.

In today's world, the most significant threats are moral, emotional, and spiritual.

Stand up for those the world pushes down

Be a shield for those who are struggling, overlooked, or mocked—whether it's the kid who's always alone, the woman facing harassment, or the man quietly carrying pain.

True protectors don't just defend with strength—they lift with compassion. Use your voice, your presence, and your courage to make others feel safe, seen, and valued.

Speak truth when silence causes harm

When lies are celebrated or someone is being torn down, don't stay quiet to protect your image. Step in. Be the one who anchors the moment in integrity—even if it costs you approval.

Create a safe space wherever you go

Let people breathe easier when you enter the room—not because you're soft, but because you carry calm strength. Let women, children, and weaker men feel secure, not scrutinized.

Intervene when something's not right.

Whether it's bullying, manipulation, or abuse, be the one who steps between danger and the vulnerable. Don't wait for someone else. Protectors don't hesitate—they move.

Guard your inner circle

Call your friends higher. Protect your brothers from self-destruction, lazy thinking, or sin. Iron sharpens iron—and sometimes that means being the one who lovingly says, "This isn't you."

Protect purity—in yourself and others.

Don't be the man who stirs up temptation. Be the one who honors boundaries, respects dignity, and sees women as daughters of God, not objects of desire.

Ask Yourself:

- **Do the people around me feel safer, stronger, and more respected when I'm present?**
- **When someone is being mocked, ignored, or mistreated—do I speak up or stay quiet?**
- **Am I using my strength to protect others... or to protect myself from discomfort?**
- **Have I allowed "normal" culture to dull my instinct to defend what's right?**

To protect is to love courageously. If you're not protecting, you're neglecting.

Try This:

- Be the first to speak up when someone is being disrespected—even if it's subtle.
- Reach out to someone who's overlooked—sit with them, listen, and affirm their worth.
- Stand between a vulnerable person and the social pressure crushing them.

Say this out loud: *"I will use my strength to shield, not to shrink. I will protect what matters."*

Protection takes guts. It takes humility. It takes action.

LEAD: Live the Call to Lead

Not for recognition. Not for ego. But because your example is already shaping someone's future.

It's about being first.

- The first to step up.
- The first to admit fault.
- The first to pursue God.

The first to walk the hard road when everyone else is still sitting on the sidelines.

Lead yourself before you try to lead others.

- If your habits are undisciplined, your leadership will be unstable. Show others what it looks like to live with order, purpose, and responsibility.

Be the first to take responsibility.

- Don't wait to be blamed—step up before it happens. Leadership means owning the mess, cleaning it up, and choosing the higher road even when it costs.

Set the spiritual tone.

- Pray first. Repent first. Worship first. A man of God leads his home, his friendships, and his community by walking with God before anyone else does.

Refuse to coast.

- When others are distracted, disengaged, or cynical, show them what it means to stay focused, hopeful, and mission-minded. The greatest leaders are consistent when others drift.

Be a thermostat, not a thermometer.

- Don't just reflect the mood of the room—set it. Bring calm when there's chaos. Strength when there's fear. Clarity when there's confusion. That's leadership.

Lead through love, not ego.

- Leadership isn't about being right—it's about lifting others. Serve. Encourage. Inspire. People follow humility far more than authority.

"Don't let anyone look down on you because you are young, but set an example for the believers in speech, in conduct, in love, in faith and in purity." 1 Timothy 4:12

Today, most young men wait to be led.

St. Joseph led with action and faith.

You don't become a leader someday. *You become a leader the moment you stop waiting for someone else to take the lead.*

Ask Yourself:

- **In what area of life am I hiding behind others instead of stepping forward?**
- **Do I lead spiritually, or follow the crowd's opinions and moods?**
- **What would change if I decided to act today?**

Try This:

- **Choose one area of chaos (in your life or family) and take initiative. No one may notice, but you will know.**
- **Begin praying aloud. Even if it's brief, lead someone —your brother, your girlfriend, a group of friends.**
- **Stop saying, "I'm not ready." You'll never feel ready. That's what faith is for.**

If you don't lead your life, someone else will. Probably the world. And it won't lead you anywhere good.

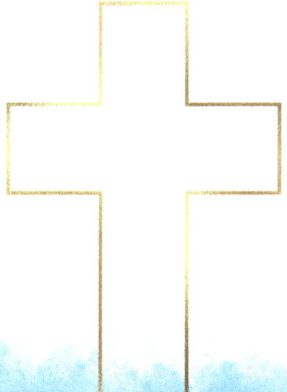

THE BRUTAL TRUTH

When men don't **_provide_**, they feel hollow.

When they don't **_protect_**, others will pay the price.

If you don't **_lead_**, your purpose will decay into wasted potential.

This isn't theoretical. It's daily.
Masculinity isn't in how you look. It's in how you live.

And that choice begins now.

Your Challenge:

Write it. Say it. Live it.

I will provide.
I will protect.
I will lead.

Not perfectly. Not easily.

But faithfully. Boldly. Daily.

The world doesn't need more passive men.

It needs you—fully alive, fully committed, fully formed into the kind of man others can trust, follow, and lean on.

Your DNA is programmed for this. It's natural. It's who God made you to be. Fully embrace it. Release it to the world.

So here's the question:

What are you waiting for?

THE
HARD ROAD

THE HARD ROAD TO SOMETHING BETTER: A REAL-LIFE CALL TO MEANING

'Let's be honest, what we're talking about isn't easy.

Becoming a man of purpose, purity, discipline, and faith in this world is like swimming upstream with weights on your shoulders.

Temptation will promise you comfort.
Compromise will beg for your attention.
And the voice of doubt will whisper, "Why bother? You're not strong enough for this."

But here's the better question: Have you looked around lately?

The world that promises you ease and pleasure is also a world drowning in anxiety, addiction, depression, broken homes, wasted potential, and lost souls. That's not judgment. That's just the truth.

And deep down, you've probably felt it. That ache that says, "There's got to be more than this."

You're not crazy. That's God calling you higher.

This Guide Isn't Just Advice. It's a Wake-Up Call.

Not from me—but from Scripture. From truth.

From the example of a man like St. Joseph, who didn't chase power or praise, but still changed the world through quiet, relentless obedience.

This message isn't new.

It's not my idea. It's the ancient path of Christian manhood.

I'm just the messenger.

"the gate is narrow and the way is hard that leads to life, and those who find it are few." — Matthew 7:14

You're the one standing at the crossroads.

One road is easy—and it leads to nowhere.

One road is narrow—but it leads to life.

You can keep going the way most guys go—drifting, dodging, delaying.

Or you can make a decision that will echo in eternity:

A life of meaning is within reach—but it will cost you your comfort. You'll have to choose:

- **Character over convenience**
- **Discipline over laziness**
- **Prayer over distraction**
- **Truth over popularity.**

The world says, "follow *your* truth."
But Christ says, "I am the way, the truth, and the life."

The world has enough passive men.
Enough performers. Enough pretenders.

What it needs... is you. Fully alive. Fully committed. Fully formed.

The only question is:

Will it be on purpose—or by default?

WHAT DOES THE BETTER PATH LOOK LIKE?

Here are signs you're stepping into the man you were created to be:

- You show up when it's inconvenient.
- You start choosing what's right over what's easy.
- You apologize when you mess up, without excuses.
- You start listening to God more than the crowd.
- You protect women, rather than objectifying them.
- You work hard, even when no one's clapping.
- You limit screen time, cut distractions, and pursue genuine relationships.
- You speak less and pray more.
- You have mentors. You're not walking alone.

WHAT TO WATCH OUT FOR: RED FLAGS THAT YOU'RE DRIFTING

- You spend more time scrolling than thinking.
- You avoid tough conversations and stay passive in relationships.
- You justify porn, casual sex, or spiritual laziness.
- You say "someday" a lot, but never start.
- You keep waiting for life to "get better" without taking any action.
- You're more influenced by culture than by your Creator.

SIMPLE, EVERYDAY STEPS TO BEGIN RIGHT NOW

Start small. Start today. Start anywhere—but start.

- Wake up on purpose. Get out of bed with a mission. Set an intention for your day.

- Start praying—even if it's awkward. A simple "God, help me become who You made me to be" is enough to begin.

- Take ownership. Clean your room. Apologize to someone. Pay your bills.

- Block time to think. No music, no phone. Just sit and ask: "Where am I going?"

- Find a real brotherhood. Seek one good friend or mentor who's trying to live with purpose. Let them help support your journey.

- Stop consuming. Start building. Replace one hour of scrolling with reading Scripture, working out, or planning your future.

- Cut ties with one thing that drags you down. You know what it is. Let it go.

YOUR CHOICE MATTERS

You won't be perfect. No one is. You'll fall. You'll get back up. You'll have good days and dark days.

But if you choose to walk this path—the path of authentic manhood—you'll have something this world can't take away:

Peace, purpose, and the knowledge that your life is building something eternal.

The culture will try to define you. But you were made to be defined by your Creator.

Choose wisely.
Choose now.
Choose your future.

CHOOSE THE JOSEPH CODE.

CLOSING
PRAYER

CLOSING PRAYER

Heavenly Father,

I come before You as I am, not as the man I pretend to be, not as the man others expect me to be, but as the man I truly am. You see everything—my doubts, my wounds, my habits, my hopes—and still, You call me. You whisper to my soul that I was made for more.

Lord, I am tired of drifting. I am tired of pretending. I am tired of the silence in my spirit when I've chased things that never satisfy. I want something real. I want to become the man You imagined when You formed me in secret. Not the version that pleases the world, but the one that honors You.

Teach me to be strong—not for power, but for protection. Teach me to lead—not with control, but with love. Teach me to sacrifice—not to impress, but to serve. Strip away the noise of this culture and speak clearly to my heart. Show me who I am—and who I can become—with You.

Let me be a man of courage in a world of compromise. A man of purity in a world of lust. A man of truth and honesty in a world of spin. Let my future family, my wife, my children, my friends, feel the blessing of the choices I make starting today.

I know I will fall. I know I will struggle. But I ask You to stay with me—to make me bold in repentance, faithful in discipline, and humble in victory. May I leave behind a hollow life and rise to something eternal. May my life shout to the world: a man of God once stood here.

Amen.

MY
COMMITMENT

MY COMMITMENT: THE MAN I CHOOSE TO BECOME

You've read the message.
You've seen the warning.
You've heard the call.
Now, the choice is yours.

This isn't about impressing anyone. It's not about being perfect. It's about stepping up—starting now.

Today, I choose to begin.

I may not have all the answers. I may still struggle.
But I will not drift through life.
I will not give my future to fear, to addiction, or to apathy.
I will not let culture define me.
I was made for more.

Today, I choose to pursue:
- **Discipline over comfort**
- **Truth over popularity**
- **Purity over compromise**
- **Faith over fear**
- **Legacy over laziness**

With God's help, I will become a man who leads, loves, protects, and provides. A man of integrity. A man of purpose. A man of God.

Write Your Name
(As a sign between you and God—no one else needs to see it.)
Name: _____
Date: _____

Prayer:
"Lord, help me walk this path with You. I give You my future. I trust You with my life. Lead me—and make me strong."

LETTER TO MYSELF

MY WHY: A LETTER TO MY FUTURE

If you're reading this, it means something stirred inside you. Maybe you're tired of drifting.

Maybe you've seen the wreckage of a life without direction. Maybe you've glimpsed what kind of man you could become—and you want to reach for it.

This is your chance to name it. To claim it. To write out your why, your reason for stepping forward.

Not for perfection. Not for applause. But for a purpose.

Journal Prompts:

1. I don't want to waste my life because...
What have you seen that breaks your heart? What do you want to avoid becoming?

2. I want to be the kind of man who...
Describe your character. What do you want people to say about you someday?

3. If I had a family one day, I would want them to say...
Think about your future wife, your kids. What would make them proud? What legacy do you want to leave?

4. I believe God is calling me to...
Is there something stirring in your spirit? A sense of responsibility, mission, or change?

5. Even when it's hard, I will remind myself that...
What truth will you hold onto when things get tough? What truth keeps you grounded?

NOW WRITE FREELY:

This is your letter to your future self. It doesn't need to be perfect. Just honest. Speak from the heart.

Dear Future Me,

_____

_____

_____

_____

_____

_____

_____

_____

_____

_____

_____

·

www.ingramcontent.com/pod-product-compliance
Lightning Source LLC
Chambersburg PA
CBHW051228120626
46547CB00013B/1561